Places in History

Versailles

Author: Antony Mason

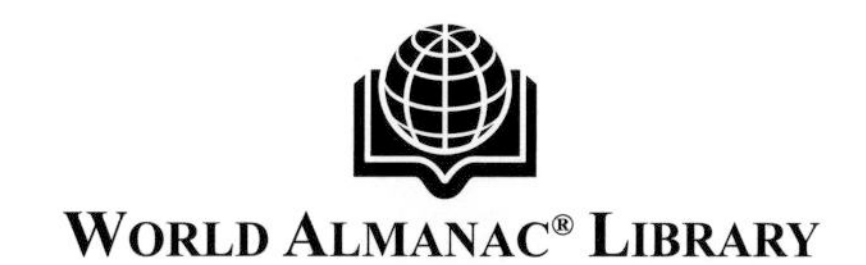

WORLD ALMANAC® LIBRARY

Please visit our web site at: www.worldalmanaclibrary.com
For a free color catalog describing World Almanac® Library's list of high-quality books and multimedia programs, call 1-800-848-2928 (USA) or 1-800-387-3178 (Canada). World Almanac® Library's fax: (414) 332-3567.

Library of Congress Cataloging-in-Publication Data

Mason, Antony.
Versailles / by Antony Mason.
p. cm. — (Places in history)
Includes index.
ISBN 0-8368-5815-8 (lib. bdg.)
ISBN 0-8368-5822-0 (softcover)
1. Château de Versailles (Versailles, France)—History—Juvenile literature. 2. Parc de Versailles (Versailles, France) —History—Juvenile literature. 3. Versailles (France)—Buildings, structures, etc.—Juvenile literature. 4. Palaces—France—History—Juvenile literature. 5. France—Kings and rulers—Dwellings—Juvenile literature. 6. Louis XIV, King of France, 1638-1715—Homes and haunts—France—Versailles—Juvenile literature. I. Title. II. Series.
DC801.V57M38 2005
944'.3663—dc22 2004056929

First published in 2005 by
World Almanac® Library
330 West Olive Street, Suite 100
Milwaukee, WI 53212 USA

Consultant: Dr. Axel Körner

Photo credits: AA World Travel Library: 1, 2–3, 19B, 24BL, 24B, Alamy: 4–5; Art Archive: 4B, 5T, 6R, 7, 8L, 8–9, 9B, 10L, 10–11, 11R, 12–13, 13T, 13B, 14, 14–15, 17T, 18T, 18–19, 19T, 20BL, 20–21, 21BL, 21TR, 21BR, 22T, 22B, 24–5, 25TR, 26R, 28, 28–9, 30T, 30–31, 32, 33L, 35T, 35B, 38L, 38R, 39R, 40, 41L; Bridgeman Art Library: 15T, 23B, 26L, 29R, 31T, 45T; Corbis: 6L, 17B, 23T, 27, 33R, 34, 36, 36–7, 37B, 42, 43L, 43R, 44–5, 45B

Printed in the United States of America

1 2 3 4 5 6 7 8 9 09 08 07 06 05

Contents

The magnificent Palace of Versailles is one of the most popular tourist destinations in France—and it is easy to understand why. Vast, grand, and filled with treasures, Versailles was Louis XIV's public showcase, attended by 7,000 courtiers. From 1682 to 1789, the palace was the principle home to the French royal family. Later in France's history, Versailles continued to play a significant role in politics. Today, the palace and gardens attract nine million visitors every year.

Fit for a King

When Louis XIV came to the throne in 1643, France was one of the world's most prosperous and powerful European states. It had by far the largest population in Europe—about 21 million people, while Spain had 7 million and the British Isles had 5.5 million. When the king assumed government, he wanted a palace that reflected his power. The site he chose was an old royal hunting lodge, 10 miles (16 kilometers) to the southwest of Paris, his capital city. In this location, there was plenty of space to build on a huge scale and to create both a grand garden filled with fountains and a park for hunting attached to the palace ground.

Louis XIV was a king who loved to be on display to his public. With the Palace of Versailles, he aimed to build a showcase of the most lavish proportions.

Building the Perfect Palace

Louis XIV's palace was the great wonder of its day. It was built to the highest standards, and no money was spared to pay the most talented architects and craftspeople that France had to offer. Work continued on the Versailles grounds during the reigns of Louis XIV's successors—Louis XV (reigned 1715–1774) and Louis XVI (reigned 1774–1792)—who developed the areas around the other, more private, palaces on the grounds, known as the Grand Trianon and the Petit Trianon.

The magnificent Hall of Mirrors is one of the palace's greatest treasures. The Treaty of Versailles was signed here in 1919, officially ending World War I.

Restoration

During the 17th and 18th centuries, Versailles (and those who inhabited it) symbolized an extravagance that was at odds with the people of France, many of whom were going hungry. This resentment contributed to the French Revolution of 1789, which later led to the overthrow of the monarchy. Versailles was saved from this turmoil and used, from 1810 to 1814, as the palace of Napoleon and then, in the 1830s, as a museum and public building. Treaties were signed at Versailles at the end of the Franco-Prussian War, in 1871, and after World War I, in 1919.

For decades, the palace has remained a rather soulless labyrinth of grand rooms. In recent years, however, a huge restoration project has been underway, and many items of furniture that once belonged to the palace have been returned to use. Each phase of restoration helps to revive the extraordinary sense of luxury, wealth, and power that Versailles once had and makes it easier to picture how it might have been in the glorious days of Louis XIV.

Ponds and water play a significant role in the style and character of Versailles. This is a view of the palace from the south.

Work began on the new palace of Versailles in 1661 and took more than fifty years to complete. Louis XIV wanted to create the grandest palace in Europe, adorned with the most spectacular gardens, lakes, and fountains. The finest architects and designers oversaw a staggering 36,000 workmen. In the 18th century, additional buildings—for housing courtiers and, more scandalously, the royal mistresses—were added to the grand site.

Modest Beginnings

In 1623, King Louis XIII built an attractive château at Versailles that became his royal hunting lodge. After his death, his son—the new king, Louis XIV—decided to make Versailles the site of his main palace. He was inspired by the palace of his ex-finance minister, Nicolas Fouquet, so much so that he employed the same architect, Louis Le Vau.

The transformation at Versailles took place in three phases. In the first phase, which began in 1661, changes were made to the

Major changes took place at Versailles in the late 17th century. Phase one included creating a massive canal to drain the swampy land and make space for the gardens (above left); phase two (above) involved building and decorating the State Apartments.

Tales & Customs — The Sun King

Louis XIV danced in a ballet called The Night ***when he was fifteen years old. Wearing a golden mask, he performed the central role of the Sun. Because of the splendors of his court and the success of his early reign, he became popularly known as the Sun King. He also liked to think of himself as Apollo, the Greek and Roman god of the Sun. There are references to the Sun and Apollo all over Versailles. In addition, Versailles itself was built to face the Sun.***

Grand Courtyard and to the front of the building. In 1667, the Grand Canal was drained to create a park. In the second phase, Le Vau created a much grander exterior. The style was neoclassical, or inspired by the architecture of Classical Greece and Rome as developed by the Italian Renaissance. The western façade was redesigned to create an impressive frontage overlooking the terraced gardens. Behind the façade, on the first floor, a series of grand new state apartments was also built. Jules Hardouin-Mansart began the third phase of building in 1678 and gave the exterior of the palace the shape it has today. Mansart designed the North and South Wings as well as many major buildings at Versailles, including the Stables and the Grand Lodgings.

Elaborate Decoration

Mansart designed Versailles's most famous room, the magnificent Hall of Mirrors, which was finished in 1684. At 246 feet (75 meters) long, it occupies almost all of the western façade of the main palace building. It is lined by seventeen large mirrors on one side, which face onto seventeen windows. The ornately carved plaster and sculptures are covered in gold, and chandeliers hang from the ceiling.

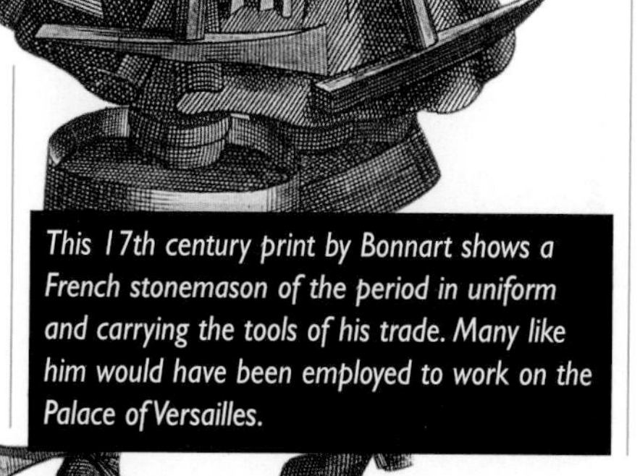

This 17th century print by Bonnart shows a French stonemason of the period in uniform and carrying the tools of his trade. Many like him would have been employed to work on the Palace of Versailles.

When Louis XIV moved into the palace on May 6, 1682, it was not finished. The chapel, for instance, designed by Robert de Cotte, was not completed until 1710, five years before the end of Louis XIV's long reign. The area around the palace was cut into huge terraces decorated with ponds and formal gardens. Large fountains adorned with sculptures formed part of this design. Beyond these gardens lay the canals and the royal hunting forest, which was ten times the size of the park today.

Water Troubles

There are more than 124 miles (200 km) of water channels, aqueducts, ditches, and pipes at Versailles. Much of the system is underground, in stone-lined tunnels. The huge capacity is necessary as Versailles's 50 fountains use 127,100 cubic feet (3,600 cubic meters) of water an hour. Versailles's water was originally supplied from the River Seine, just 7.5 miles (12 km) away. The trouble was that the water had to run uphill to a height of 52 feet (16 meters) in order to reach Versailles. It was moved uphill by a huge pump built at Louveciennes: 14 huge waterwheels operating 221 pumps, which pushed the water up the hill to reservoirs near Marly. Built over a period of thirty years from 1681, the "Marly machine" was considered to be one of the wonders of the world in Louis XIV's day, even though it could provide only enough water to run all the Versailles fountains for three hours. Various improvements were tried but none were completely successful until much later. Louis XIV liked to think he could solve any technical problem, but the problem of supplying water to Versailles bugged him for the rest of his life.

The aqueduct at Marly that stored and transported water to Versailles was proclaimed as one of the great wonders of Louis XIV's day.

Wives, Mistresses, and Culture

In 1670, Louis XIV built a palace for his mistress, Madame de Montespan, on the grounds of Versailles, clearing a village called Trianon to make room for it. Because this palace was deco-

Tales & Customs — An Opportunity Missed

The failure to supply Versailles's fountains with adequate water has been a source of regret for centuries. In 1841,* François-René de Chateaubriand, a French writer, *wrote that it was a ". . . shame that Louis XIV, by force of necessity, shocked by those calls for economy, which are so often the downfall of the grandest plans, ran out of patience; France would otherwise have possessed today the greatest monument on Earth."

This 18th-century painting shows the Queen's Hamlet. Louis XVI's wife, Marie-Antoinette, was perceived as haughty, snobbish, and extravagant by the people of France. However, she found peasant life so appealing that she had a mock village built, where her courtiers dressed up in country attire—a common fashion among the European aristocracy of the time.

rated with blue and white Chinese porcelain, it was called the "Trianon de Porcelaine." After the death of the Queen in 1863, Louis XIV married another mistress, Madame de Maintenon. For her, he demolished the Trianon de Porcelaine, and in 1687, replaced it with a building faced with marble, called the "Trianon de Marbre." A vigorous period of building came later in the 1760s, under the direction of Louis XV's former mistress, the great intellectual and friend of the arts, Madame de Pompadour. Part of the exterior of the main palace was rebuilt, and the magnificent Opera House was added to the North Wing in 1770. The King also built an intimate palace for Madame de Pompadour called the "Petit Trianon." The larger Trianon de Marbre now became known as the "Grand Trianon." As country life was fashionable among the aristocracy, Louis XVI's wife, Marie-Antoinette, liked to get her courtiers and ladies-in-waiting to dress as farming folk and carry out country activities in a fake rural village, known as the Queen's Hamlet, built nearby.

Much of the Grand Trianon, such as these columns that flank a checkered walkway, is decorated with rose-pink marble.

Rescued for the Nation

In 1810, after the French Revolution, Napoleon Bonaparte redecorated the Grand Trianon for Empress Marie-Louise in the new "Empire Style." He also completed the North Wing of the main palace, which had never been finished.

After the overthrow of the Bourbon monarchy in 1830, King Louis-Philippe converted the two wings into a Museum of French History, demolishing many of the apartments of the princes and courtiers to make room for it. Some changes have since been made to the Palace, but what visitors see today has essentially remained the same for more than 150 years.

CHAPTER 2 Versailles through History

Versailles is famously known as the place where Louis XIV conducted his extraordinary public life. It also served as a stage for Louis XV's famous mistress, Madame de Pompadour, and as a playground for the frivolous queen Marie-Antoinette. But Versailles is also remembered as the place where the peace treaty that ended World War I was signed—a treaty some see as so one-sided that it was one of the causes of World War II.

This ornately decorated spear was carried by the guards of Louis XIV.

Rise of the Sun King

Louis XIV was the son of Louis XIII and Anne of Austria. When Louis XIII died in 1643, Louis XIV was just five years old, so while he remained a minor (until the age of thirteen), his mother ruled as regent, assisted by her chief minister, Cardinal Jules Mazarin. This was a troubled period for Europe, which was devastated by the Thirty Years' War (1618–1648), a late consequence of the Reformation. At the end of the war, France emerged as the strongest power in Europe, but heavy taxes caused the nobility to revolt in the civil war known as the Fronde (1648–1652). Mazarin taught the young Louis XIV how to conduct wars and run the country and instilled in him the concept of absolute power and the "divine right of kings"—the belief that he had been chosen by God to rule.

When Mazarin died in 1661, Louis XIV announced that he would rule in his own right. He was assisted by a very able new chief minister, Jean-Baptiste Colbert (1619–1683). Colbert reformed the tax system, encouraged trade, and helped to develop industry. As a result, France grew wealthy—and so too did Louis XIV. It was at this time that Louis XIV began his grand building projects, first at the royal palaces in Paris and then Versailles. The first twenty years of Louis XIV's rule were his finest. The court moved to Versailles in 1682.

Military Pride and Religious Conflict

War was an essential part of any great king's role, and he was flattered by his generals that he was good at it. Louis XIV liked to review the army at parades and

Time Line

1623	Louis XIII builds a hunting lodge at Versailles.
1661	Work begins on the transformation of Versailles under Louis XIV.
1663	The royal menagerie is moved to Versailles.
1667	Work begins on the Grand Canal at Versailles (completed in 1679).
1668	Work begins on the new palace of Versailles.
1670	Louis XIV builds the Trianon de Porcelaine for Madame de Montespan.
1682	The royal court and parts of the aristocracy take up residence at Versailles.

This statue depicts Louis XIV dressed as a Roman emperor crushing a rebel during the Fronde revolt.

took credit for victories. Most of his wars were connected to claims of inheritance from the Habsburgs, the ruling family of Austria, Hungary, and Spain. Louis was a Bourbon, the family that had ruled France since 1589; but both his mother and his wife were Habsburgs.

Louis XIV was anything but a private man. In the above illustration, he is receiving visitors from the alcove of his chambers at Versailles.

Like much of Europe, France had been torn apart by religious conflict in the 16th century, as Catholics fought with Protestant Huguenots in the Wars of Religion (1562–1598). Some peace was achieved by the Edict of Nantes of 1598, which allowed freedom of worship to the Protestants. But Louis XIV, for foreign-policy reasons and to better control his country wanted France to be Catholic. In 1685, he withdrew the Edict of Nantes. As a result, about 400,000 Huguenots, most of whom belonged to France's professional and intellectual élite, emigrated.

The French had been developing settlements in Canada since 1604, claiming the land for themselves as "New France." In 1663, Louis took control over the territories, and numerous settlers from France began to arrive. French explorers, meanwhile, headed south and carved out a vast territory for France, which in 1682 was named after Louis XIV: Louisiana. This area was far larger than the modern state of Louisiana.

A Quieter Sanctuary

Louis XIV died in 1715, outliving his son and one of his two grandsons. Because his other grandson became king of Spain, France was ruled by his brother, the Duc d'Orléans, until Louis XV (the great-grandson of Louis XIV) was old enough to formally take the throne in 1723.

1683 Queen Marie-Thérèse dies at Versailles. Louis marries his mistress, Madame de Maintenon.

1687 Louis XIV builds the Trianon de Marbre (Grand Trianon) for Madame de Maintenon.

1715 Louis XIV dies at Versailles at the age of 77.

The Duc d'Orleans ruled France as regent until Louis XV was old enough to rule France on his own. In this 18th century painting, the young Louis receives a school lesson from one of his teachers.

Louis XV was a much less publically visible king than Louis XIV, which meant that Versailles became a much quieter place than in earlier times, with much less ceremony and public entertainment. Unlike his predecessor, Louis XV preferred to retreat to the privacy of the Grand Trianon to dine with friends. The old royal courts of law, known as the parlements, were gatherings of the nobility, who had historically tussled with the king. Louis XIV had ended up suppressing them. The Duc d'Orléans, however, restored them in 1718. The parlements became the focus of opposition to the king in the late 18th century. Toward the end of Louis XV's reign the parlement of Paris was once more suppressed, and Louis assumed power as absolute monarch.

The Seven Years War

Wars still raged throughout Europe over who should succeed whom. Louis XV's gifted chief minister, Cardinal Fleury, managed to keep France out of the War of Austrian Succession (1740–1748), but unfortunately, France did become involved in the highly complex Seven Years War (1756–1763). Although fought mainly in central Europe, British and French interests

Time Line

- **1715** Following the death of Louis XIV, the court abandons Versailles and moves to Paris.
- **1723** Louis XV succeeds the throne upon the death of the Duc D'Orleans.
- **1725** Louis XV marries the Polish princess Marie Leszczynska.
- **1757** Robert Damiens attacks the king with a penknife at Versailles and wounds him. Condemned to death, Damiens is tortured with red-hot pincers and boiling oil, and then torn to pieces by horses.
- **1762** The Petit Trianon is built for Madame de Pompadour, but she dies before it can be put into use.

clashed due to their overseas possessions. As a result, France lost control of Canada and Louisiana, as well as parts of India. France, once the proud owner of valuable overseas territories, lost much wealth and prestige.

The Enlightenment

The 18th century was a period of scientific discovery and invention. Scientists were making progress in many areas, including physics, medicine, and astronomy, by applying careful methods of observation, reason, theory, and experiment. A similar approach was taken to philosophy and political thought, concerning such ideas as personal freedom, equality, and democracy. This movement was called the Enlightenment. In France, it was led by a group of thinkers and scientists known as the philosophes. They had close contact with the court at Versailles; Madame de Pompadour actively encouraged the philosophes to compile the great book of the Enlightenment, entitled the *Encyclopédie*. One of its contributors was the writer Voltaire, who described Versailles as "a masterpiece of bad taste and magnificence."

Louis XV was a much less public king than his great-grandfather, Louis XIV.

By the end of Louis XV's reign, France was virtually bankrupt. There were numerous reasons, including the costs of war, the loss of overseas territories, and royal extravagance. Although France's finances recovered a little in the final years of his reign, when Louis XV, died he left a debt of 4 billion livres (about 13.7 billion U.S. dollars, in modern money).

Choosing Sides and Going It Alone

In 1775, the people of thirteen colonies of North America began a rebellion against their British rulers, and the following year issued their famous Declaration of Independence. The result was the American Revolution. One contributor to the Declaration of Independence was the American politician and inventor Benjamin

1768 Queen Marie dies at Versailles.

1770 The future Louis XVI marries Marie-Antoinette in a spectacular celebration at Versailles; the Opera House, designed by Jacques-Ange Gabriel, is completed for the occasion.

1774 Louis XV dies at Versailles at the age of 64.

Louis XV built the Petit Trianon for his mistress, Madame de Pompadour, who was a great patron of the arts and the Enlightenment thinkers.

Franklin, who became the American ambassador to Versailles. He helped to persuade France to support the Americans against Britain with troops, money, and naval ships. After the last British surrender in 1781, Franklin and others negotiated for peace; in the resulting Treaty of Paris (sometimes called the Treaty of Versailles), signed in 1783, Britain recognized the independence of the United States of America.

This painting shows a group of counter-revolutionaries singing during the 1789 French Revolution. The French Revolution was an uprising of the people against their extravagant monarchy.

In 1788, the government of France went bankrupt. This problem was caused by political conflicts and because the expense of funding wars had caused massive debts. Meanwhile, the tax system, which was needed to raise funds, was in chaos. All the while, the royal court continued to spend lavishly, which only incited resentment among the people. A harvest failure added to poor people's anger, as they now faced rises in the price of bread. The State Generals were summoned to Versailles in 1789. The Commoners, however, who formed a majority, gathered at the royal tennis court in the town of Versailles on June 20. They swore that they would not disband until their demands were met by Louis XVI. On July 9, the State Generals declared themselves the National Assembly.

Revolution

The people of Paris were furious about the concentration of troops in the capital and the general economic situation. On July 14, 1789, they attacked the Bastille, an old prison that was a symbol of royal oppression. This event has been described as the start of the French Revolution.

On October 5, 1789, craftsmen from Paris and their wives marched on Versailles, demanding bread and for the royal court to return to Paris where they could be watched by the citizens. The following day, rioters broke into the palace and massacred the guards defending the Queen's Suite. Only the help of the Marquis de Lafayette prevented the massacre of the royal family. After trying to leave the country,

Time Line

1774 Louis XVI is crowned king of France.

1775 Marie-Antoinette builds the Hameau de la Reine.

1788 France becomes bankrupt.

1789 The French Revolution forces Louis XVI and his family to leave Versailles for Paris. The people attack the Bastille.

1792 Versailles is stripped of much of its contents. France is declared to be a Republic. France declares war against Austria and Prussia, beginning the French Revolutionary Wars.

1793 Louis XVI is executed by guillotine in January; Marie-Antoinette is executed in October.

Louis XVI and Marie-Antoinette were eventually executed for treason in 1793. In 1792, the National Convention declared France to be a Republic—a country ruled by the people. Meanwhile, the new government in Paris began to fear that French opponents of the Revolution, who had fled abroad, would persuade foreign enemies to attack.

In April 1792, war was declared against Austria and Prussia. This was the start of the French Revolutionary Wars. The Revolution profoundly transformed French society by making all citizens equal, limiting the influence of religion on public life, liberating the economy, and introducing administrative reforms all over France. The changes were mostly to the advantage of the middle classes.

This portrait shows Louis XVI's frivolous queen Marie-Antoinette in hunting attire.

Attacks on the Revolutionary movement from the outside and inside the Republic caused its leader Maximilien Robespierre to use terror to control the situation, resulting in the execution of about 35,000 people and leading France into a state of turmoil. Robespierre was eventually overthrown and executed in 1794, and power was handed over to a new government. This marked the start of a more orderly and peaceful period.

This 18th century cartoon illustrates October 5, 1789, when a crowd consisting mainly of women stormed the palace of Versailles, calling for food and for the royal family to return to Paris.

1793 Robespierre leads the Reign of Terror. He is eventually overthrown and executed in 1794.

1795 The Dauphin (Crown Prince) dies in mysterious circumstances. The Directory results in a period of stagnation in revolutionary France.

An Emperor or a King?

Napoleon Bonaparte was just thirty years old when he seized control of France. A successful general in the Revolutionary Wars, Napoleon launched a series of wars, known as the Napoleonic Wars, across Europe. Napoleon restored Versailles and redecorated the Grand Trianon in the new "Empire" style.

This style was neoclassical and intended to symbolize the harmony of all things under Napoleon's leadership. The rise of Napoleon gave Europe twenty-five years of turmoil and war, but also an important period of modernization, ending with his final defeat in 1815.

The victorious Allies believed the best way to restore order to France was to reinstate the monarchy of the Bourbons. So, Louis XVIII was placed on the throne. Under the new king, the North Wing at Versailles was completed. Louis was succeeded by his brother Charles X. His tyrannical regime was overthrown by the Revolution of 1830, and he was replaced by the Duc D'Orleans, Louis-Philippe. Louis-Philippe's constitutional monarchy led to a financial crisis and provoked a revolution in 1848 that forced him to abdicate. France became a republic once again.

In 1852, a nephew of Napoleon organized a coup against the republic and took the title of Emperor Napoleon III. In 1870, a dispute with Prussia led to war, and France was rapidly overrun.

In 1870, Versailles became the headquarters of the Prussian army, the residence of the King of Prussia, and a hospital. In January 1871, a peace treaty was signed at Versailles. At the same time, the German states unified as one nation, and William I of Prussia was proclaimed the first Emperor of Germany in the Hall of Mirrors. The Third Republic was formed during the Franco-Prussian War. The Opera House of Versailles became the setting for meetings of the National Assembly, and in 1875, a Congressional Chamber was built in the South Wing.

This neoclassical painting shows Napoleon Bonaparte on horseback. Napoleon did a great deal to restore Versailles, such as renovating the Grand Trianon.

- **1810** Empress Marie-Louise, second wife of Napoleon, takes up residence in the Grand Trianon.
- **1820** Building work on the North Wing is completed.
- **1833** Louis-Philippe opens the Museum of French History in Versailles.
- **1870** Versailles becomes the Prussian headquarters during the Franco-Prussian War.
- **1871** A peace treaty signed at Versailles ends the Franco-Prussian War. William I of Prussia is declared the first Emperor of Germany in the Hall of Mirrors.
- **1875** The Congressional Chamber is built in the South Wing.

This painting illustrates the signing of the Treaty of Versailles in the Hall of Mirrors in 1919. The Treaty stipulated that Germany should surrender territory and pay compensation for provoking World War I.

The Treaty

During the early 1900s, alliances between European states became strained as they challenged each other for control of overseas territories. Matters came to a head in 1914, when World War I began, as Austria-Hungary and Germany declared war on Serbia and France. Much of the fighting took place in eastern France and Belgium, where Germany confronted the Allies (France, Britain, and the United States). Hundreds of thousands of soldiers and civilians died. The war ended when an armistice was reached in November 1918. The following year, leaders of the Allies met at Versailles to negotiate a peace treaty. The Treaty of Versailles essentially blamed Germany for the war and demanded heavy penalties. Germany had to hand over most of its overseas territories, it had to return Alsace-Lorraine to France, and it had to pay war reparations. The Treaty of Trianon, between the Allies and Hungary, followed in 1920. Some people say that the humiliation of the Versailles Treaty and the hardships caused by reparations contributed to the rise of the Nazi party in Germany and, thus, to World War II (1939–1945).

Peaceful Times

Charles de Gaulle, the former leader of the Resistance during World War II, was elected president of France in 1959. Under De Gaulle, Versailles once again resumed its place in French public life, when a wing of the Grand Trianon became a residence of the French head of state. Since then, Versailles has hosted many international heads of state, including Nikita Khrushchev, Leonid Brezhnev, and Mikhail Gorbachev of the Soviet Union; John F. Kennedy and Richard Nixon of the United States; and Queen Elizabeth II of Great Britain.

In this photograph, United States president John F. Kennedy (middle floor, fifth from left) attends a concert at Versailles alongside French president Charles de Gaulle.

1919 The Treaty of Versailles establishes the peace settlement after the end of World War I.

1966 The Trianon-sous-Bois becomes a residence of the French president.

1999 On December 26, 10,000 trees on the grounds of Versailles are uprooted by hurricane-force winds.

CHAPTER 3 Exploring Versailles

Versailles is a big place. First, there is the palace itself, with a string of rooms to visit. In the magnificent gardens and park are dozens of beautiful fountains and statues, plus two smaller palaces, the Grand Trianon and the Petit Trianon, and Marie-Antoinette's mock country hamlet, the Hameau de la Reine. Outside the palace gates lie the historic tennis court as well as the Stables, which house the carriage museum. Seeing everything takes at least a whole day, so it is wise to plan a visit carefully.

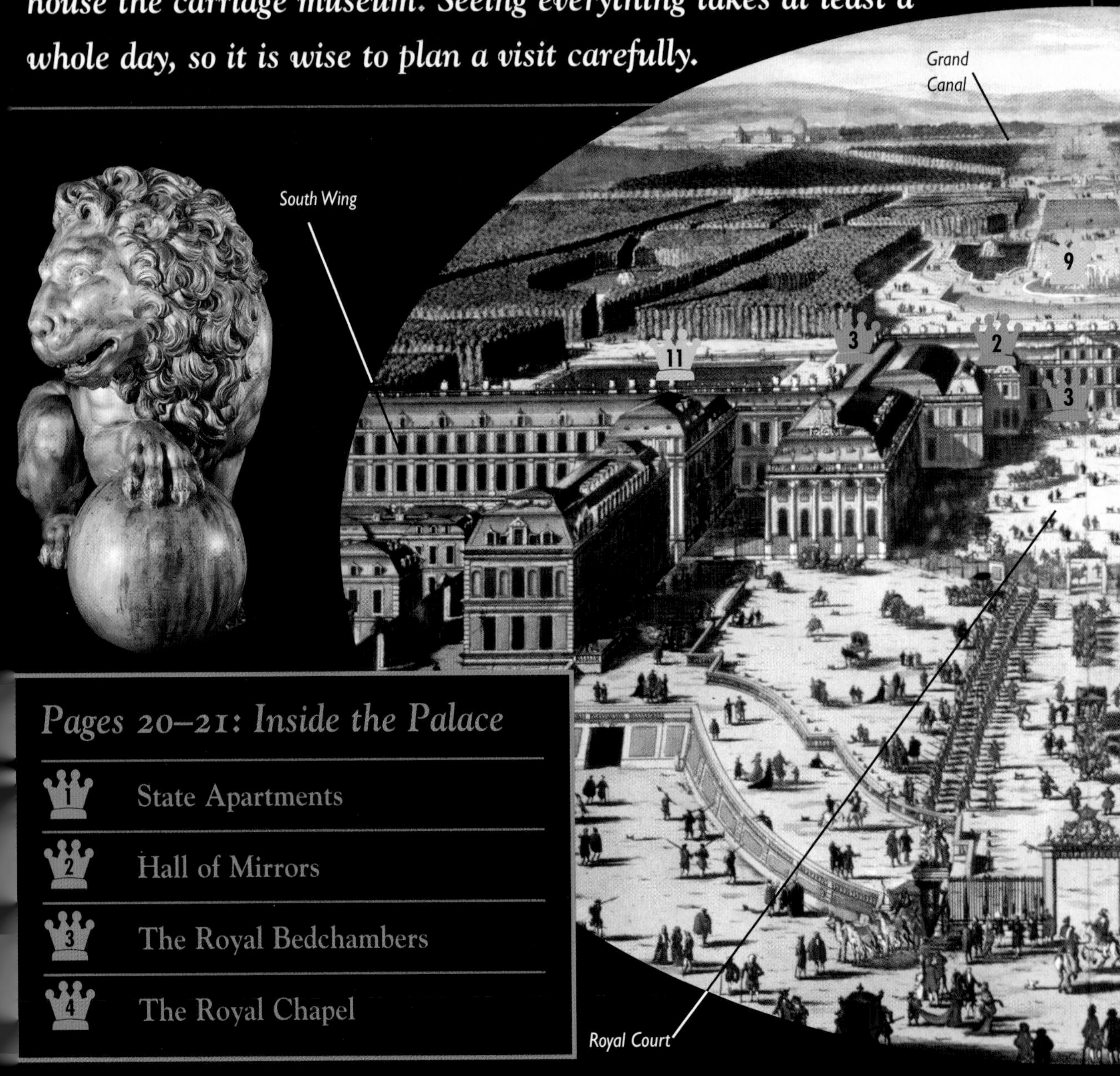

Pages 20–21: Inside the Palace

1. State Apartments
2. Hall of Mirrors
3. The Royal Bedchambers
4. The Royal Chapel

Pages 22–23: The Grand Trianon and the Petit Trianon

 Grand Trianon

 Petit Trianon

 Queen's Hamlet

 Temple of Love

* *Carriage Museum, out of view*

Pages 24–25: The Gardens and the Park

 The Formal Gardens

 The Neptune Fountain

 The Orangery

 Carriage Museum

State Apartments

The six State Apartments were originally designed to impress visitors. The rooms are named after figures from ancient mythology. The Salon of Hercules was specially designed by Robert de Cotte in 1710 to 1730 to contain a painting by Veronese called *Christ at the House of Simon the Pharisee*. It remains the greatest work of art on display at Versailles. At the end of the series is the Salon of Apollo, which served as the throne room of the Sun King.

The Salon of Apollo is one of the Palace of Versailles's six ornately decorated State Apartments.

Hall of Mirrors

Since it was completed in 1684, Jules Hardouin-Mansart's Hall of Mirrors has been considered one of the most famous rooms in Europe. Originally solid silver furniture added to the glittering effect, but Louis XIV had to melt it down to help pay for the country's wars. The seventeen mirrors are actually made up of 578 smaller panes. The ceiling depicts events from the first seventeen years of Louis XIV's reign.

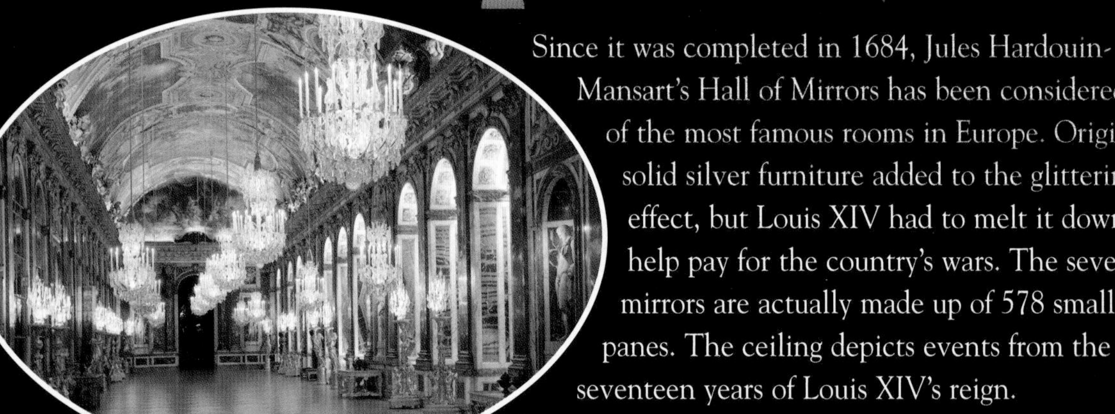

The Hall of Mirrors is one of the palace's most popular rooms. Beautiful paintings adorn the ceiling and walls, while mirrors and chandeliers glisten.

The Royal Bedchambers

The reigning queen had a separate suite of rooms, facing south and overlooking the gardens. This was where she could hold court. The most magnificent room was the Queen's Bedchamber, into which only her closest courtiers were invited. It was also where the queen gave birth to her children, watched by an audience. The Queen's Bedchamber has been restored to how it would have looked at the time of Marie-Antoinette. The king had another private suite of rooms overlooking the courtyards. They included the King's Bedchamber, at the very center of the building. Luxuriously decorated, this is where Louis XIV began and ended his day. He actually slept in another room called the Petite Chambre du Roi.

The rich gold and red brocade hangings in the Queen's Bedchamber have been restored to how they looked during Queen Marie-Antoinette's reign.

The Royal Chapel

Dedicated to St. Louis, the chapel was completed in 1710, toward the end of Louis XIV's reign. It is the tallest part of the palace, with an interior space soaring to 82 feet (25 meters). The king, who attended Mass daily as part of his court ritual, would sit on the tribune on the upper level, overlooking the courtiers below.

The Royal Chapel in the North Wing of the palace is dominated by grand neoclassical pillars and archways.

This carved lion detail is from a chair that was made in 1681 for the royal chapel at Versailles. It was a gift from Louis XIV.

The mirror salon from the left wing of the Grand Trianon has been decorated with furnishings from the 19th century.

Grand Trianon

The unique mixture of stone and pink marble that covers the exterior of the Grand Trianon was Louis XV's idea. These days, part of the building, the Trianon-sous-Bois, is reserved for the use of the president of France. The interior of the Grand Trianon was originally decorated in luxurious style by Louis XIV and Louis XV and then refurbished by Napoleon for his wife, Empress Marie-Louise, in 1810. The interior retains a mixture of all these styles.

Completed in 1768, the Petit Trianon was inhabited by many royal mistresses.

Petit Trianon

The Petit Trianon was built between 1763 and 1768, in the Greek style that was fashionable at the time. Louis XVI gave it to Marie-Antoinette when he came to the throne in 1774, and she used it as a private mansion. The interior was redecorated by Empress Eugénie, wife of Napoleon III, in the 1860s, in the style of Louis XVI. The Petit Trianon dining room was created for Louis XV so he could eat his dinner among friends and away from public view. Through an ingenious design, the tables could be lowered through the floor, into the kitchen below, where they could be reloaded with food.

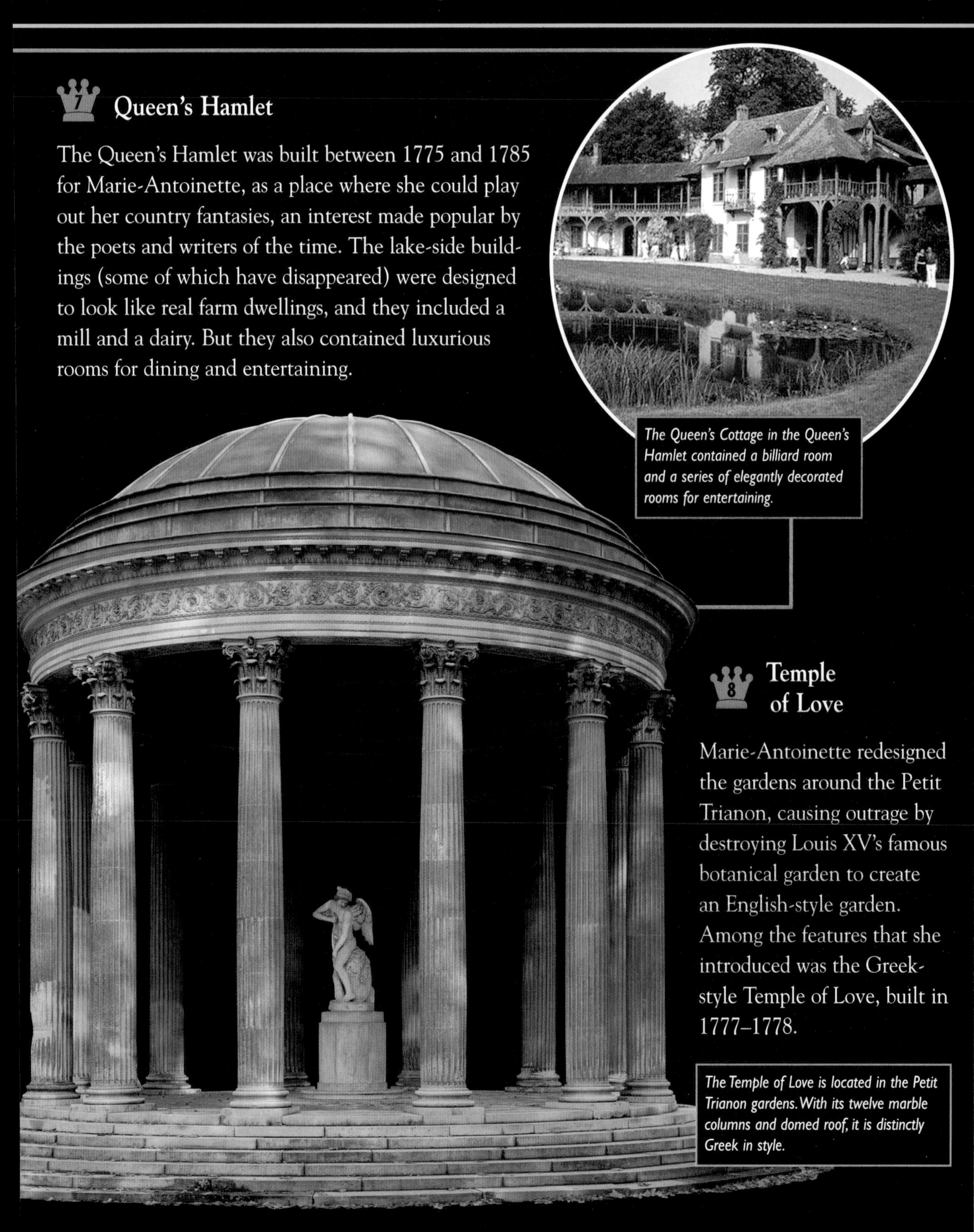

7 Queen's Hamlet

The Queen's Hamlet was built between 1775 and 1785 for Marie-Antoinette, as a place where she could play out her country fantasies, an interest made popular by the poets and writers of the time. The lake-side buildings (some of which have disappeared) were designed to look like real farm dwellings, and they included a mill and a dairy. But they also contained luxurious rooms for dining and entertaining.

The Queen's Cottage in the Queen's Hamlet contained a billiard room and a series of elegantly decorated rooms for entertaining.

8 Temple of Love

Marie-Antoinette redesigned the gardens around the Petit Trianon, causing outrage by destroying Louis XV's famous botanical garden to create an English-style garden. Among the features that she introduced was the Greek-style Temple of Love, built in 1777–1778.

The Temple of Love is located in the Petit Trianon gardens. With its twelve marble columns and domed roof, it is distinctly Greek in style.

* Carriage Museum, out of view

The Formal Gardens

The garden nearest the palace is laid out on a set of descending terraces that are divided neatly into geometric shapes made up of pools and patterns of clipped hedges. The garden features a total of 13 miles (21 km) of hedges. Designed by Le Nôtre, this is a classic example of a French-style formal garden.

This painting shows Louis XIV taking a walk with his entourage in front of the immaculately manicured formal gardens.

The Neptune Fountain

There are 32 ponds and 50 fountains at Versailles. Many of these are decorated with sculptures depicting Greek and Roman deities and mythical figures. One series of fountains was designed to tell the story of Apollo—the Greek Sun god—rising in his chariot at dawn and ending his daily cycle at the Grotto of Thetis, where he was attended to at dusk by nymphs. One of the most spectacular fountains is the Bassin de Neptune, which has 50 spouts and produces 147 different effects.

The Neptune Fountain continues a running theme at Versailles of depicting Greek and Roman gods and goddesses.

The Orangery

Oranges were the height of luxury in Louis XIV's time. Beneath the terrace outside the South Wing is the Orangery, in which hundreds of orange trees and palm trees were protected in individual tubs from the winter cold . In the summer, the trees were—and still are—wheeled out and displayed on the terrace. The steps on either side are called the Great 100-Step Staircases. The Orangery also contains King Louis XIV's marble bathtub.

The Orangery was built to contain not only orange trees and palm trees but also many other exotic plants.

The Carriage Museum is located in the building that once contained the royal stables and grooms' quarters.

Carriage Museum

The two massive stables (the Grande Écurie and the Petite Écurie) outside the palace gates, on the Place d'Armes, were not just stables for seven hundred horses, but also barracks and accommodations for grooms, pages, and musicians. The Grande Écurie contains the Carriage Museum, with coaches collected by King Louis-Philippe. One of the oldest was used in the marriage of Napoleon to Marie-Louise in 1810.

Many of the great events in French history took place at Versailles, and some of these events were colored by court intrigues and by the complex private lives of the French kings. The last French king, Louis-Philippe, may have abandoned the throne in 1848, but since that time, Versailles has remained one of France's great palaces. Leaders on the world stage have continued to come through its doors.

Louis XIV ruled France for 72 years—a longer reign than any other major European monarch.

Louis XIV

Because Louis XIV was the first child of Louis XIII and Anne of Austria after twenty-two years of marriage, he was nicknamed Louis Dieudonné, or Louis Godgiven. After the death of France's chief minister, Mazarin, Louis XIV was deemed old enough to assume the throne—at which time he decided to take over complete control of government. Obsessed with detail, Louis was devoted to his duty as king. He worked tirelessly and treated himself like public property that should always be on show to the nation. Believing himself to be second only to God, Louis was both kindly and ruthless. His weakness, however, was flattery: His ministers, generals, courtiers, and mistresses knew that they could get their way by telling him what he wanted to hear.

Marie-Thérèse of Austria

The daughter of Philip IV of Spain, Marie-Thérèse was Louis XIV's cousin, and almost exactly the same age as him. Their marriage in 1660 was designed to heal the wounds of the Thirty Years War (1618–1648), during which France had supported the Protestant powers against Catholic Spain. It also brought together the Bourbon family of France with the Habsburgs of Spain and Austria. Louis met Marie-Thérèse only three days before the wedding, and he soon lost interest in her, at which time she had to learn to share her husband with his mistresses. She bore him six children, only one of whom survived, a son called Louis. Their son, the Grand

Marie-Thérèse, wife of Louis XIV, is shown here with her son Louis, known as the Grand Dauphin, who died before his father.

Tales & Customs—King and Saint

Louis XIV descended from Louis IX, also known as Saint Louis (reigned 1226–1270), a crusader-king famed for his honesty, virtue, and sense of justice. Some people believed that Louis XIV inherited healing powers—passed to him from his ancestor—during his coronation ceremony. At Versailles, the sick would gather in the Stone Gallery, hoping that Louis XIV, in his procession to the Chapel, might touch them and cure them.

Dauphin, or Crown Prince, died in 1711, four years before his father, and never became king of France. Marie-Thérèse died in 1683, a year after the royal court had moved to Versailles.

Louis XIV's Mistresses

Louise de La Vallière was just sixteen when she became the King's mistress in 1660. Rising from humble origins and with a slight limp, she was a celebrated beauty. Louise was a center of attention at the great festival at Versailles, called the "Pleasures of the Enchanted Island" in 1664. She fell from favor when the king turned his attentions to Madame de Montespan, and she retired to a convent. Madame de Montespan entered court as lady-in-waiting to Marie-Thérèse and was mistress to Louis XIV from 1667 to 1679. A vivacious beauty, she was the leading lady of Versailles for more than a decade, a position she jealously guarded against all rivals to the King's attention. Madame de Montespan's reputation was wrecked by her involvement in the Poison Scandal—in which it was revealed that she had participated in black-magic séances with various unsavory characters in Paris.

The French kings were famously public with their infidelities. Besides lavish gifts of the finest clothes and shoes (such as this delicately embroidered leather shoe from Louis XIV's reign) many French kings gave their mistresses their own accommodations.

This detail from the ceiling painting in the Hall of Mirrors documents France's renewed alliance with the Swiss against the Habsburgs.

Madame de Maintenon was governess to the children of Louis XIV and Madame de Montespan and became mistress to Louis XIV beginning in 1675—especially after Madame de Montespan fell from favor. She married the king in a secret nighttime ceremony in October 1683, three months after the death of Queen Marie-Thérèse. She had a strong influence on Louis in the later part of his life.

Architects and Craftsmen

A leading French architect of his day, Louis Le Vau designed the château of Vaux-le-Vicomte for Nicolas Fouquet, before being recruited by Louis XIV to rebuild the Louvre in Paris. Le Vau also masterminded the first two phases of rebuilding at Versailles. Another member of Fouquet's team, Charles Le Brun, was appointed Chief Painter to the King and took over the decoration of the main rooms of Versailles. One of his greatest works is the ceiling painting in the Hall of Mirrors.

A botanist, architect, and painter, the multitalented André Le Nôtre was responsible for the gardens of Versailles. He became the royal gardener in 1637, a post that his father and grandfather had both held before him. Louis XIV was particularly fond of Le Nôtre. Le

This Prussian engraving of officers of the castle guard during the era of Louis XIV (1638–1715) gives a clear indication of the importance placed on fashion during the period.

Tales & Customs—On the Throne

Almost every aspect of Louis XIV's life was on display. He would even receive guests while sitting on the toilet. In fact, it was considered a great honor to be invited to visit the king in the bathroom. The kind of toilet used by Louis XIV was called a close stool—a kind of chair with a hole in the seat and a potty underneath. The king's was particularly ornate and comfortable, decorated with Japanese scenes on black lacquer and fitted with a seat upholstered in velvet.

Nôtre, however, was extremely modest and refused any special honors.

Courtiers

The rituals of court life at Versailles were aimed at maintaining Louis XIV's power over the different ranks of French society. Louis XIV surrounded himself with able ministers and officials, but their appointment was based on favors. To succeed, a courtier had to catch Louis's eye and hope to be granted the honor of some post, such as Officer of the Bedchamber, Officer of the Wardrobe, or Officer of the Household. The most favored courtiers were permitted to attend the most intimate moments of Louis's daily life, such as the levée (getting up in the morning). Court life was expensive. The aristocrats had to maintain households in Versailles, with staff, stables, and carriages; they had to keep up with the latest fashions; and they had to have plenty of money for gambling. The worst thing that could happen to a courtier was to fail to be noticed. Louis's most damning criticism about a courtier was, "I do not know him." Louis used this combination of favoritism and expense—and his vast network of spies and informers—in order to keep his court under control.

Louis XV

Louis XV (1710–1774) was the successor to his great-grandfather Louis XIV. Because both his father and his grandfather had died, Louis XV came to the throne at the age of just five years old. His reign lasted fifty-nine years. In 1725, at the age of fifteen, he married Marie Leszczynska, daughter of the king of Poland. They had ten children, but only seven survived. Louis XV was shy and a far more private man than Louis XIV; he spent much of his time in retreat from the court in his private apartments and at the Grand Trianon. Louis XV's reign was marred by the loss of many of France's overseas territories in North America and India during the Seven Years War and by the mounting debts that paved the way to the French Revolution. He died of smallpox at Versailles.

Louis XV was king of France from 1723 to 1774. The Duc d'Orleans ruled on his behalf until Louis XV's fourteenth birthday.

Madame de Pompadour

Madame de Pompadour was Louis XV's mistress from 1745 to 1750, but she continued to play an important role at court and in politics after that year. She encouraged Louis to take part in the Seven Years War (1756–1763) and so was blamed for the losses suffered by France. But at court she was welcomed for reviving intellectual debate and organizing festivities, dinners, and balls. She was a patron of the arts and a supporter of many writers and philosophers of the Enlightenment. She also had a great influence on tastes and fashion at court.

Madame de Pompadour was a colorful and flamboyant 17th-century figure. Her life was even celebrated in the twentieth century. This 1933 poster advertised an operetta about her.

Louis XVI

The last of the great French kings to rule from Versailles was Louis XVI (1754–1793). The grandson of Louis XV, he was generally popular but suffered from indecision and from being married to the deeply unpopular Marie-Antoinette, who had a strong influence on his rule and choice of ministers. His reign was dominated by the growing financial crisis that led to bankruptcy in 1788. His refusal to accept reform led to increasing hostility in the early days of the revolution. He lost all sympathy by encouraging opponents of the Revolution abroad and by attempting to flee to

This lithograph from 1870 shows an aristocratic scene from King Louis XVI's day. Wealthy people spared no expense on the finest fashions. This displeased the common people who could barely afford food for their families.

Tales & Customs — The Diamond Necklace Affair

The lover of the Cardinal of France, Comtesse de Lamotte, persuaded a jeweler that she was buying a diamond necklace on Marie-Antoinette's behalf. However, instead of giving the necklace to Marie-Antoinette, the Comtesse gave it to her husband, who promptly ran off to London and sold it. The story made the news and caused public indignation by exposing Marie-Antoinette's extravagant lifestyle.

Austria in June 1791. His support for the counterrevolutionary war launched by his Austrian nephew, Francis II, in 1792, led to his arrest for treason and to his execution in 1793.

Marie-Antoinette

The daughter of Maria Theresa and Francis I of Austria, Marie-Antoinette (1755–1793) married Louis XVI when she was fourteen and he was fifteen. Young and arrogant, she made herself unpopular in the royal court through her favoritism and frivolity. She had little patience for the formal etiquette of Versailles and made no effort to conceal her boredom. She preferred to retreat with her friends to the Petit Trianon and her fake rural farming village, the Hameau de la Reine. She was widely disliked by the French public. It was rumored that when she was told that the starving poor of Paris were rioting because they could not afford bread, she responded, "Let them eat cake!" Accused of instigating Louis XVI to promote Austrian resistance to the French Revolution, she received little sympathy as she was taken for execution at the age of thirty-seven, in October 1793, dressed in rags, in an open cart, jeered by the crowd. In these final traumatic months, however, she behaved with remarkable courage and dignity.

This 19th-century engraving shows Louis XVII, son of Louis XVI and Marie-Antoinette. When his parents were taken to prison, the young Louis was also imprisoned. Some people believe that he mysteriously disappeared from prison. However, recent DNA tests on what is believed to be his heart appear to support the claim that he died in prison at the age of ten.

The "Lost Dauphin" Louis XVII

The second son of Louis XVI and Marie-Antoinette, Louis became dauphin at the age of eight, just before the Revolution. In 1792, he was imprisoned with his family in Paris' Temple Prison. After the execution of his father, he was proclaimed king by royalists, but he probably died of tuberculosis in prison. Rumors suggested that he had escaped, giving rise to the legend of the "lost dauphin" and a host of pretenders claiming to be the true heir to the throne of France.

Napoleon Bonaparte

Napoleon Bonaparte (1769–1821) shot to fame as a dynamic young general during the French Revolutionary Wars. In 1799, he took control of France as consul. He upheld many of the ideals of the Revolution, giving opportunities to talented people and introducing a modern set of laws. There was a brief period of peace in 1802, then he resumed his military campaign, attempting to create a single European empire by conquering Italy, Austria, Spain, and Germany. But he was defeated by British naval leader Horatio Nelson at the Battle of Trafalgar in 1805. Napoleon moved to Versailles after his marriage in 1810. He refurbished the Grand Trianon for his new bride, and he gave the Petit Trianon to his sister, Pauline. Napoleon's campaign against Russia in 1812 was a disaster, and the French were defeated in 1814. Napoleon abdicated and was sent to the Italian island of Elba. He escaped in 1815, returned to France, and raised an army, but he was defeated at the Battle of Waterloo in June. He was then sent to the remote island of Saint-Helena in the South Atlantic, where he died in 1821. Napoleon's second wife, Marie-Louise, was the daughter of Francis II of Austria. She married Napoleon in 1810, when she was nineteen and he was forty-one. Their marriage united the Austrian Empire with France. She refused to join Napoleon when he was exiled to the Italian island of Elba, and in 1814, she left Paris for Austria with their son. After Napoleon's death in 1821, she remarried and became Duchess of Parma, in Italy.

This detail from a painting shows the hand of Marie-Louise of Austria (Napoleon's second wife) holding the imperial crown.

King Louis-Philippe

A descendant of Philippe I, Duc d'Orléans (brother of Louis XIV), Louis-Philippe was chosen to become king of the French when Charles X abdicated during the Revolutions of 1830. Having supported the Revolution, he was considered by the middle classes to be one of them and so was called "the Bourgeois King." He restored Versailles, and turned a wing of the palace into the Museum of French History, while he and his family lived in the Grand Trianon. He introduced reforms, but his refusal to extend the vote to the middle classes caused resentment. He was forced to abdicate during the

Tales & Customs—The First Air Passengers

On September 19, 1783—witnessed by Louis XVI, Marie-Antoinette, and about 130,000 spectators—the brothers Joseph and Étienne Montgolfier attempted the first hot-air balloon flight. When they launched the balloon, from the courtyard in front of the palace of Versailles, its three passengers were a duck, a rooster, and a sheep. The animals landed safely after eight minutes in the air and a flight of 2 miles (3.2 km).

Widely regarded as one of the greatest military figures in history, Napoleon Bonaparte emerged from the chaos of the French Revolution to lead France as emperor from 1804 to 1814.

Revolution of 1848 and retired to Surrey, England, where he supposedly called himself "Mr. Smith."

Napoleon III

A nephew of Napoleon I, Louis Bonaparte was elected president of the Second Republic in 1848, after the Revolution that had removed Louis-Philippe. In 1852, he took the title of emperor, and he ruled as Napoleon III until France lost the Franco-Prussian War in 1871. In 1853, he married Eugénie de Montijo, who renovated the Petit Trianon during the 1860s. Napoleon III also restored and replanted the gardens of Versailles.

Charles de Gaulle

In 1940, during World War II, Germany invaded France. When this happened, the Minister of War and army colonel Charles de Gaulle fled to Britain to lead the French Resistance. Before the recapture of France after D-Day, de Gaulle was made leader of the French government. He was called back to be head of government in 1958, and he presented a new constitution and became president beginning in 1959, but he retired after the commotions of May 1968. De Gaulle understood the symbolic role of Versailles and adapted the Trianon-sous-Bois as a presidential palace.

Charles de Gaulle was the leader of the Free French Forces in World War II. In 1958, after a constitutional crisis, he became the first president of France's Fifth Republic.

Versailles began as a pleasure palace. It was first a lodge for hunting ("the sport of kings") and then it functioned as a scene for the representation of the powerful French monarchy. Throughout its history, Versailles has been the setting for plays, opera, and music. Today, the palace has a busy schedule of exhibitions, concerts, and performances, including spectacular summer shows combining music and its famous fountains.

The Pleasures of the Enchanted Island

Louis XIV held spectacular festivities at Versailles, even before the palace was completed. In 1664, just two years after work had begun on the gardens of Versailles, Louis XIV hosted one of the most spectacular parties in history. It was called "The Pleasures of the Enchanted Island." Queen Anne, the King's mother, was the guest of honor, but Louis was also celebrating his love for his young mistress, Louise de La Vallière. On the first night, the park was lit by torchlight and many thousands of candles. In an open-air theater, Louis himself played the lead role in a play called *Orlando Furioso*, entering on horseback, followed by a procession of dozens of costumed performers, animals from the menagerie, and the glittering chariot of Apollo. The play—about an enchanted island—was made magical through special effects, and it culminated in a huge fireworks display. The week continued with a jousting tournament and, by night, theater, concerts, dances, and ballet, and outdoor feasts served by staff dressed as fauns and wood-nymphs.

Many events at Versailles close with an awe-inspiring fireworks-and-light-show display, as captured in the photograph above.

Tales & Customs—French Literature

The three great French dramatists—Molière, Corneille, and Racine—all worked at Versailles for Louis XIV. Molière produced a wide range of different types of court entertainment, but he is best known for his comedies. Corneille and Racine wrote tragedies. Another famous author and poet closely involved with the Versailles of Louis XIV was La Fontaine, who is best known for his collections of animal fables.

This 17th-century engraving shows a stage set for a theater production at Versailles. Plays by the great French dramatists Molière, Corneille, and Racine were performed on temporary stages at Versailles, at the bidding of Madame de Maintenon and Madame de Montespan.

Lively Evenings at the Palace

Events were part of court life—a way of keeping the court loyal and entertained. Throughout the winter season, when the court was at Versailles, there was a daily program of entertainment: plays by the leading dramatists of the time, and music played by the three palace ensembles. Music, in fact, accompanied all events in the State Apartments, in the gardens, on the Grand Canal during boating excursions, and even on hunting trips.

Three times a week, an evening event took place in the State Apartments. The evening began at 6 P.M. with a concert. Then there was dancing, card games, gambling, food, and drink. The evenings ended at 10 P.M., when the company went to watch the royal family dine at the Grand Couvert, held in the Antechamber of the King's Suite.

This 1670 watercolor fan painting shows a boatload of Louis XIV's guests at a festival on the Grand Canal.

Special Occasions

Each year there were special occasions—such as the stately procession of the Knights of the Order of the Holy Spirit, held on January 2—that ended in a ceremony in the Royal Chapel. Big occasions, including royal weddings, celebrations of military victories, and visits by foreign ambassadors, were celebrated in grand style. One of the most famous was the marriage of the future Louis XVI and Marie-Antoinette in 1770, for which 6,000 invitations were issued and about 200,000 members of the public showed up to witness the three-day spectacle. The Opera House was completed for the occasion. It was ingeniously constructed so that the auditorium floor could be raised to the stage level to create a spectacular dining room and ballroom and then lowered again for opera performances. The whole park was magically illuminated to create a kind of opera of light.

Fountains, Music, and Fireworks

The tradition of festivities continues today with regular concerts held at the Opera House, the Royal Chapel, and the Salon of Hercules. A series of special exhibitions is mounted each year in various apartments, galleries, and halls, each celebrating some aspect of Versailles's history and its cultural contribution to France and the world at large. But the palace's most famous special events take place in the gardens during summer, each specially designed to evoke the glorious days of royal Versailles. The Grand Musical Waters is a tour of the fountains, accompanied by music of the 17th and 18th centuries. The tour takes visitors around the route that Louis XIV himself devised to see the best viewpoints over the gardens, which include nine major fountains and twelve woodland groves. The finale takes place at the Neptune Fountain, where ninety-nine water spouts shoot 33 feet (10 m) into the air, accompanied by the music of Handel.

The grand diva of rock, Tina Turner, performs on stage at Versailles. Many other contemporary performers have staged concerts at the palace.

Even more spectacular, however, are the Grand Nocturnal Waters, which take place on Saturday nights in July.

Beginning at sunset, visitors are taken on a magical musical tour of the garden and groves to see the fountains, all beautifully illuminated. The music of Lully is

Tales & Customs—No Time for Lunch

Louis XVI and Marie-Antoinette might have survived the Revolution if they had been willing to hand over power to the National Assembly. In June 1791, they were given an opportunity to flee to safety in Austria. Dressed as servants, they fled under the cover of darkness. However, for comfort they took a large, slow carriage, and Louis insisted on stopping for a picnic, wasting crucial time. News of their escape traveled fast. At Varennes, 40 miles (65 km) short of safety, they were recognized and taken back to Paris.

Lighting is often used to dramatic effect in combination with the fountain system during performances at Versailles, as seen in this picture of a scene from an opera performed in the 1990s.

prominently featured, because he wrote music especially to accompany Louis XIV's outdoor festivities. The music and settings unfold in a drama of four themes: music for nocturnal festivities, music for sleep, the music of nightmares (evoking demons and witches), and, lastly, music for prayer and reflection. Complementing the music are performances by costumed theatrical groups, musicians playing authentic instruments, fire-eaters, and palace guards in the uniforms from the era of Louis XIV. The program ends with a fireworks display—just as Louis XIV would have wished it.

The Big Summer Show

For more than forty years, Versailles has put on a spectacular outdoor late-summer show at the end of August and beginning of September. Stands are erected beside the Neptune Fountain with enough seating for 50,000 people, and some of the audience can even watch from boats floating in the fountain's huge pond. Each year the show has a different theme related to Versailles. In 2004, for instance, the show was based around the story of the Chevalier de Saint-George, a noble in the court of Marie-Antoinette. He was unusual because his father was a plantation owner and his mother a black slave; he was born on the Caribbean island of Guadeloupe. The Chevalier de Saint-George was a celebrated musician, composer, swordsman, and horseman, and the show combined all these elements. The show was designed and choreographed by the famous horse trainer and showman Bartabas, who incorporated into the show fifty Lusitanian horses, now stationed at the Grande Écurie, along with a large team of percussionists, actors, and dancers—and, of course, fireworks.

The Opera House built by King Louis XV at Versailles often hosts lavish balls and operas. In this picture, a model poses in a gown that fits in with the dramatic architecture.

Versailles is magnificent. But it is still just a shadow of what it once was. In the days of Louis XIV, it was filled with exquisite furniture, paintings, tapestries, books, and vases, and it astonished the world with its sumptuous luxury. Above all, it was full of people, dressed in costumes of exceptional lavishness. Today, we need imagination to restore in our mind's eyes the full impression of Versailles as it once was.

Source Material

There is no shortage of documentation about the palace of Versailles. In the palace collection alone, there are 6,000 paintings, 1,500 drawings, and 15,000 engravings. There are architects' drawings, paintings,

This intricate design for the Queen's Theater in the Petit Trianon was designed by the architect Richard Mique in 1786.

engravings, maps, and written descriptions that tell us how the palace was built and how it changed over time. There are public records, printed books, newspaper articles, and private diaries that tell us what went on

This photograph of the bedchamber of Marie Antoinette, located in the Queen's Apartments, clearly conveys just how extravagant the Queen's tastes were.

there. Bills show us what items were purchased and how much was spent. All these give us insight into the history of Versailles.

Palace of an Absolute Monarch

Louis XIV wanted to create the biggest, most impressive palace in Europe—the palace that all other kings would try to copy, the palace that would leave visitors gasping with astonishment. That was its purpose from 1661 to 1789. But we can also look at Versailles and see how it was a symbol of extravagance and waste. While the royal family and nobles frittered away their time and money at Versailles, the middle classes had to pay heavy taxes, and the poor barely had enough to eat. The grand rooms of Versailles may be splendid, but they are also echoing, empty rooms. An obvious target for the revolutionaries of 1789, Versailles remained a rather awkward reminder of the past swept aside by the French Revolution. But it was too grand, too famous, and too much of an achievement to demolish. After the Revolutions of 1830, King Louis-Philippe tried to resolve this awkwardness by making Versailles into a museum of French history. It has since become a National Palace, with its Congress Hall used for parliamentary sessions and with official functions held in the State Apartments.

Amidst uncertainty about the future purpose of Versailles, King Louis-Philippe turned the palace into a museum of French history.

The Treasure Hunt

The French authorities have decided to do whatever is possible to recreate how Versailles looked when it was in its full glory. One way of doing this is to recover as many of its original pieces of furniture and other objects as possible. In 1962, a government decree ordered

Tales & Customs—But What's It Worth?

The best pieces of furniture in Versailles did not come cheap. The most expensive item bought by Louis XV was a roll-top desk (a prototype for all roll-top desks), made by one of the leading furniture makers of the day. It cost 65,000 livres, which in today's money would be about US $220,000 (UK £120,000). All the furniture of Versailles was sold during the Revolution of 1793. While a few pieces have since been recovered, most remain in private hands.

that all objects from Versailles in French museums should be restored to the palace. Unfortunately, many of the most valuable items from the palace are not in French museums. After an auction in 1792, some were sold to private individuals, and many of them went abroad. The Sèvres porcelain of Louis XVI and Marie-Antoinette, for instance, is now in the British royal collection. Experts have been keeping a close eye on auction rooms around the world; furniture from Versailles has been bought in the United States, London, and Tokyo.

Under the Magnifying Glass

With their wealth and power, Louis XIV, Louis XV, and Louis XVI could afford the best craftspeople in the world. Their furniture is made of beautiful exotic woods, decorated with gold and semiprecious stones, all shaped, carved, and polished to perfection. Their clocks represented not only the finest craftsmanship, but the leading edge of science and technology of their day. The porcelain plates from which they ate were produced to a standard that has never really been matched, even today. Their clothes were made of the finest and most expensive cloth, which was then tailored, lined, and embroidered to the most exquisite standards.

Each of these priceless items represents many hundreds of hours of work. Versailles was at the tip of a complex system of trade, involving many people, from craftworkers, shopkeepers, and merchants to the laborers cutting the flax required to make linen. The complexity of this world can be detected in many of the objects displayed at Versailles.

This distinctive porcelain plate from 1823 has a scene from the period of Louis XVI painted on it. It was made at the royal porcelain factory at Sévres.

The Finest Garb

An interesting example is the portrait of Louis XIV by Hyacinthe Rigaud. In this picture, Louis is standing in front of his throne, at the age of sixty-two, in full regalia. He is wearing full court dress, with a lace ruff and cuffs, silk breeches, silk stockings with garters, and high-heeled shoes with diamond-studded buckles. His ermine-lined mantle is in royal blue, embroidered with the fleur-de-lis (iris), the symbol of the French royal family. Also shown are the symbols of kingship—the crown; the sword of Charlemagne (the 8th-century king of the Franks and, later, Roman Emperor), which represented his role as protector of the Church and the kingdom; and the scepter, the ancient symbol of royalty.

The Kings' Passions

Louis XV was fascinated by science, technology, and craftwork. He carved ivory and experimented with cookery, and he would even make his own ironwork. Perhaps the most extraordinary evidence of his interest in science and technology can be seen in the astronomical clock found in the clock cabinet of his apartments. It can show the time, the phases of the Moon, the movement of the planets, and the date until the year 9999. Completed in 1754, it took a clockmaker and an engineer twelve years to complete.

Tales & Customs—Ghostly Apparitions?

In 1901, two English women claimed to have had a strange experience near the Petit Trianon. They said they came to a cottage beside a gazebo where they saw a man in 18th-century costume with a heavily pock-marked face and a woman in old-fashioned dress sitting and sketching. Later, they discovered that a cottage, gazebo, and bridge had all existed in that area in 1789 but did not exist in 1901. Also, they said that the woman had looked just like a painting of Marie-Antoinette.

Louis XIV surrounded himself with finery, from the rich fabrics of his robes to the fine exotic woods of his furniture. This painting by Hyacinthe Rigaud captures something of the King's love of material things.

This cabinet from the time of Louis XVI is decorated with insects and plants made from feathers and insect wings, and inlaid with gold.

Like many noblemen of the time, Louis XVI was an avid collector of things that interested him. This is perhaps best illustrated in a cabinet that he had made from gold coins in 1788 (now in Louis XV's apartments at Versailles). The surfaces of this cabinet are decorated with birds, butterflies, and plants, all made from feathers and beetles' wings. Such objects give us glimpses into the character of the kings who lived at Versailles, and the way a powerful monarchy represented itself.

About 9 million people visit Versailles every year, two-thirds of whom are foreigners. Of these visitors, 3 million tour the house, and 6 million visit the grounds. In other words, Versailles is one of the top visitor attractions in France. Looking after Versailles and all of its visitors is, therefore, a major undertaking. And the best advice to any visitor, especially in the busy summer season is: Get there early!

Drivers of horse-drawn carriages, who offer rides to visitors in the park, are just some of the many people who make a living working at Versailles.

Running Versailles

Some 600 people are employed to look after Versailles. This includes 363 guards, who patrol the rooms and the grounds; 48 gardeners; 11 curators, who look after and maintain the palaces and their precious contents and who also carry out historical research; 3 architects who are specialists in the conservation of historic buildings; 18 art restorers; 40 lecturers and guides; and 8 fountain technicians. In addition, there are cleaners, carpenters, plumbers, and staff running the restaurants and shops, the boat rental, the minitrain, and the horse-drawn carriages. Versailles belongs to the French nation. It is, therefore, run as a public institution, like any of the major national galleries and museums. For ten years now, however, the palace has had its own administrative organization that works to preserve and improve the famous site.

The forty-eight gardeners who work at Versailles are constantly occupied with tending the palace's extensive gardens.

Open to the Public

The Palace of Versailles is closed on Mondays and certain French public holidays. Otherwise, it is open every day of the year. Many local people treat the park of Versailles as a public space. Access to much of the park is free, but visitors have to buy a ticket to gain access to the formal gardens next to the palace. Both are open for much longer hours than the palace, virtually from dawn to dusk. It is possible to visit Versailles as a day trip from Paris, but it is a good idea to set out early because there is so much to see. Only half of Versailles's treasures are on display to the general public. The rest are in safekeeping.

The Guides at Versailles

The tour guides at Versailles are incredibly knowledgeable about Versailles's past, cleverly weaving the history in with references to what you can see before you. They also keep their audiences entertained with anecdotes and stories, such as the one associated with a painting that clearly illustrates Napoleon's contempt for the Catholic Church. Napoleon invited Pope Pius VII to his coronation, during which he was to be crowned emperor of France. However, when the pope went to place the crown on the new emperor's head, Napoleon snatched the crown from his hands and placed it upon his own head. This showed that Napoleon believed that the pope had no legitimate right to crown him because in the "new France" the Church had no power over the state.

A typical day at Versailles. Visitors stroll near the Fountain of Latona, the mother of Apollo. A complete trip on foot around the gardens and park can take hours.

Myths and Legends — The Daily Spectacle

The court of Louis XIV was obsessive about detail, and each day was planned to the last minute, from waking to going to bed at night. Virtually every aspect of Louis XIV's life was a public performance, attended by selected courtiers. Who was allowed to assist in which event was controlled by a rigorously and jealously guarded order that depended on winning the King's favor.

The conservation team at Versailles is constantly busy maintaining and preserving the palace buildings, furnishings, and gardens. On top of this continuing work, there have been a couple of major incidents that have damaged the palace complex, including the explosion of a bomb in 1978 and a hurricane that toppled 10,000 trees in 1999.

Restoration work at Versailles is ongoing. Any such work is carefully directed by art historians and archaeologists. About twenty years ago, the renovation of more than eighty rooms was funded by the French government. This restoration work permitted the ground-floor apartments of the Dauphin and Dauphine to be opened to the public.

Time and Nature

With 3 million visitors passing through the palace every year, along with the threat of damage by weather and insects, keeping Versailles in good condition is a constant challenge. This is the daily task of Versailles's team of eighteen art restorers, and there are many factors they must take into account. When the Treaty of Versailles was signed in 1919, the palace and the park were in a dilapidated state. In the 1920s, with the assistance of grants from the American oil tycoon John D. Rockefeller Jr., modern restoration began, and it has continued ever since. Two magnificent projects have set high standards for restoration at the palace. The Queen's Bedchamber was restored to the sumptuous style of Marie-Antoinette in 1975, and the King's Bedchamber was restored in 1980. The real triumph of these projects was the restoration of the beds and their elaborate hangings, which give some indication of the richness of cloth and textiles that surrounded the royal court in the 17th and 18th centuries.

The extraordinary Fountain of Enceladus—which depicts a mythical giant struggling under a pile of stones—was renovated

The King's Bedchamber was renovated in 1980 to look exactly as it did while Louis XIV was king of France.

and regilded in 1998, along with more rooms of the apartments of the Dauphin and Dauphine. The main project on which historians are focusing recently is the restoration of the Hall of Mirrors, starting with the floor and then moving on to the carved and painted wall decorations.

Disaster Strikes

Renovations became more pressing after several disasters took place at the palace in the 20th century. These included a bomb explosion inside the palace on June 26, 1978, which caused widespread damage. The bomb had been planted by terrorists demanding independence for Brittany. They targeted Versailles because they believed it was a symbol of French oppression. Then, in 1999, hurricane-force winds knocked down about 10,000 trees in the park of Versailles. These two events caused major setbacks for the staff that works on caring for and restoring the palace.

The photograph above shows one of the many trees felled by the hurricane of December 1999.

Tales & Customs — The Royal Grill

The inner courtyard of the palace was originally protected by a golden fence and gate that kept the public away from the courtyard beneath the windows of the royal apartments. Known as the Royal Grill, this fence was torn down during the Revolution. The plan, under the current restoration program, is to reinstate it. However, the restoration of the Royal Grill is a controversial project, because the equestrian statue of Louis XIV will have to be moved to make room for it.

abdicate: to give up the role of king or queen in order to make way for a new monarch to take the throne.

absolute power: power held completely by the king or queen. That is, the power is not shared with anyone else; the monarch rules entirely alone.

Apollo: ancient Roman and Greek God of the Sun, also traditionally associated with music and poetry. Louis XIV was often compared to Apollo; this is one reason why he was nicknamed the "Sun king."

aqueducts: long bridge-type structures that hold and carry water to towns and cities.

aristocracy: the highest-ranking social class, which includes people with titles, such as duke, marquis, earl, viscount, baron, knight, and esquire.

armistice: a temporary wartime truce or peace brought about by agreement between the opposing sides.

bankrupt: legally proven to lack the money to pay debts.

château: the French word for a large French country house or castle.

civil war: a war in which the two warring sides are citizens of the same country.

coronation: a ceremony in which a new king or queen is officially crowned.

courtiers: attendants or advisors to a king or queen who are present at a royal court.

D-Day: the day during World War II (June 6, 1944) when the Allied Forces invaded Normandy in northern France to attack German troops stationed there.

dauphin: the eldest son of the King of France; also called the crown prince.

dictator: a ruler who has total and tyrannical control of a country.

divine right of kings: a theory that proposes that certain kings were chosen by God to rule and that they were answerable to no one but God.

Edict of Nantes: the law issued on April 13, 1598, by Henry IV of France that granted French Protestants (also known as Huguenots) rights and freedoms in the predominantly Catholic nation of France.

empire: a large group of states ruled by a single monarch or ruling territory.

Empire style: the neoclassical style of clothing, architecture, and decorative arts that developed in France in the early 19th century during Napoleon's rule. It was meant to visually reflect the harmony of all things under Napoleon's leadership.

Enlightenment: the intellectual and philosophical movement that developed in Europe during the late 17th and 18th centuries that emphasized the use of reason to make sense of things.

extravagant: going above and beyond what is necessary, for the sake of fashion or whim.

façade: the front of a building.

French Revolution: the overthrowing of the French monarchy (1789–1799) by the people of France who revolted against the extravagance of their royal leaders. This marked the end of the French royal lineage and the emergence of democracy and the right of the common people.

Grand Trianon: a small palace built in 1687 by Louis XIV for his mistress, Madame de Maintenon, originally called the Trianon de Marbre. Trianon was the name of the town cleared specifically to make way for the first Trianon palace to be built (the Trianon de Porcelaine).

menagerie: a collection of wild animals kept in captivity for public entertainment. The menagerie at Versailles was established by Louis Le Vau at the request of Louis XIV.

monarchy: a state or country in which supreme power is held by a single, hereditary ruler.

Napoleonic Wars: the series of French campaigns led by Napoleon Bonaparte against Austria, Russia, Great Britain, and other European countries.

neoclassical: having to do with an art and architectural style that was strongly influenced by the art and architecture of Classical Greece and Rome.

nobility: the privileged social class; also called aristocracy.

parlements: the thirteen regional royal courts in 18th century France that were empowered to register royal decrees before they became law. In this capacity, the parlements opposed royal initiatives that they believed threatened the freedom of the people.

Petit Trianon: the small palace built by Louis XV for his mistress, Madame de Pompadour. (See also: Grand Trianon)

philosophes: a group of intellectuals who had a lot of influence over the French government in the 18th century.

Prussia: the former kingdom of Germany situated in what is now southern Lithuania, part of Russia and northeastern Poland.

regent: a person who rules a state on behalf of a reigning monarch who is too young to rule in his or her own right.

Reign of Terror: the period during the French Revolution (1793–1794) during which a few men tried to govern France and carried out many executions of presumed enemies of the state.

reparations: compensation for war damage paid by a defeated state to the victor of a war.

republic: a state ruled by its citizens rather than by a monarch.

séances: meetings during which people hold hands in a circle and attempt to make contact with the dead.

successor: a person who takes over something from another person, such as a new king taking over from the former king.

Sun King: the nickname given to King Louis XIV because of the success of his reign and the magnificence of his court.

Third Republic: the republican government that ruled France following the collapse of the empire of Napoleon III in 1870.

treason: the crime of betraying one's country.

treaty: a legally-binding agreement between countries or states.

tribune: a raised platform on which a speaker stands to address a gathering.